Your Food

Sally Hewitt

Crabtree Publishing Company

www.crabtreebooks.com

Crabtree Publishing Company

www.crabtreebooks.com

Author: Sally Hewitt
Editors: Jeremy Smith, Molly Aloian
Proofreaders: Adrianna Morganelli, Crystal Sikkens
Project editor: Robert Walker
Production coordinator: Margaret Amy Salter
Art director: Jonathan Hair
Design: Jason Anscomb
Prepress technician: Katherine Kantor

Activity pages development by Shakespeare Squared
www.shakespearesquared.com

Picture credits: Alamy: pages 8, 20 (bottom); Bridget Ringdahl:
pages 14 (top), 20 (top), 22; Corbis: pages 3, 5, 14, 16 (top), 17;
Fairtrade: pages 24, 25 (top); istockphoto.com: pages 13 (bottom),
19 (bottom); Martin Luther King Junior School: page 15; Mossbank
School, Shetland: page 12 (top); Plan International: page 19 (top);
SIGN: pages 10-11; Shutterstock: pages 6-7, 9, 12 (bottom left and
bottom right), 12 (center), 21, 22, 23, 25 (center right and bottom);
Stephanie Alexander Kitchen Foundation: page 18
We would like to thank Bridget Ringdahl for use of photographs
and her text relating to Rocklands Primary, South Africa.
Every attempt has been made to clear copyright. Should there
be any inadvertent omission, please apply to the publisher
for rectification.

Library and Archives Canada Cataloguing in Publication

Hewitt, Sally, 1949-
      Your food / Sally Hewitt.

(Green team)
Includes index.
ISBN 978-0-7787-4099-5 (bound).--ISBN 978-0-7787-4106-0 (pbk.)

      1. Food--Juvenile literature. 2. Environmental responsibility--
Juvenile literature. 3. Sustainable living--Juvenile literature. I. Title.
II. Series: Hewitt, Sally, 1949- . Green team.

TX355.H49 2008   j641.3   C2008-903493-7

Library of Congress Cataloging-in-Publication Data

Hewitt, Sally, 1949-
   Your food / Sally Hewitt.
      p. cm. -- (Green team)
   Includes index.
   ISBN-13: 978-0-7787-4106-0 (pbk. : alk. paper)
   ISBN-10: 0-7787-4106-0 (pbk. : alk. paper)
   ISBN-13: 978-0-7787-4099-5 (reinforced lib. binding : alk. paper)
   ISBN-10: 0-7787-4099-4 (reinforced lib. binding : alk. paper)
   1. Food--Juvenile literature. 2. Environmental responsibility--
Juvenile literature. 3. Sustainable living--Juvenile literature.
I. Title. II. Series.
   TX355.H4875 2009
   641.3--dc22

2008023291

Crabtree Publishing Company

Published in Canada
Crabtree Publishing
616 Welland Ave.
St. Catharines, Ontario
L2M 5V6

Published in the United States
Crabtree Publishing
PMB16A
350 Fifth Ave., Suite 3308
New York, NY 10118

Contents

Paul →

← Jane

What is on the menu?

What kind of food do you choose to eat? Do you choose food that is good for you, or any food as long as you like the taste? You can try to choose tasty food that is good for you and good for the planet. Become part of the **Green Team!**

Good for you

A healthy diet

In order to be healthy and fit, we need to eat different foods. Food can be put into five groups. All of these groups are important for the body. A balanced diet is one that includes all the food groups.

We need to eat more food from some of these food groups than others. Use the plate on the right to get the correct balance of what you should eat. The smaller the section on the plate, the less you need of that type of food.

Fruit and vegetables provide:
- vitamins
- minerals
- carbohydrates
- fiber

Bread, cereal, rice, potatoes, and pasta give us:
- carbohydrates, the food your body uses for energy.
- B vitamins
- calcium
- iron
- fiber

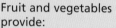

Meat, fish, and beans give us:
- protein
- iron
- vitamins
- minerals

Foods containing fat and sugar give us energy, but we should not eat too much of these types of food.

Milk and dairy products give us:
- calcium
- vitamins
- protein

These children are enjoying a healthy and delicious lunch.

Challenge!

- Is the food you choose to eat every day good for you?
- What can you do to improve your diet?

Good for the planet

To join the Green Team you also need to make sure you eat food that has been properly prepared and is good for the world around you as well as tasty to eat.

Fairtrade

Cheap food for us can mean the farmer's family goes hungry. Food that carries the Fairtrade label means that the farmer who produced it has been paid a fair amount of money.

Organic food

Chemicals that kill insects can kill plants and animals, too. Choose food grown without dangerous chemicals.

Food miles

Some food has traveled from the other side of the world for you to eat. You can choose to buy food grown near where you live and help to cut down food miles.

Packaging

Choose food that comes without much packaging, or in packaging that can be reused, **recycled**, or will break down quickly.

Action!

Find out if your lunches are good for the planet. Is the food:

- Fairtrade?
- **organic**?
- local and **seasonal**?

If not, ask your school to make changes.

Giang

Time for a picnic

If you are planning a picnic or taking a lunch to school, think before you pack your food and drink. Use washable containers you can use again and again so you do not have to keep throwing away packaging.

Energy is used to make unnecessary packaging. It has to be thrown away. Then more energy is used to get rid of the packaging.

Some fruits have their own natural wrapping.

Challenge!

- Collect all the packaging used in your class's lunch boxes for one week.
- For one week, try not to use any wrapping that cannot be reused, recycled, or put in the **compost** bin.
- Compare the piles of packaging for the two weeks.
- Keep up the challenge and reduce packaging week by week. Can you get it down to zero?

Fruits and vegetables

You can either eat the skins of fruits and vegetables or peel them and put them in the compost bin. Result—no waste!

Drink tap water rather than bottled water to cut down on packaging.

Drinks

Buy a big container of milk or juice instead of many small ones. Pour some into a washable, reusable bottle for your picnic or packed lunch.

Sandwich box

Put your sandwiches in a small container in your lunch box. Fill it with homemade coleslaw, pasta, or salad for a change.

Yogurt bowl

Get a reusable bowl for your desserts. Fill it with fruit salad or yogurt from a big container.

Action!

Make your own picnic lunch

Bake pancakes, muffins, or banana bread (see below).

Make a fruit salad

Make more than you need for one meal. Freeze or store the extra food or share it with friends.

⚠ Remember to ask for adult help when baking.

Banana bread

Preparation time: less than 30 minutes
Cooking time: about 1 hour

Ingredients
2 cups all-purpose flour
1 teaspoon baking soda
¼ teaspoon salt
½ cup of butter
¾ cup brown sugar
2 eggs, beaten
2 ⅓ cups Fairtrade bananas (the softer the better), peeled and mashed

Method
1. Pre-heat the oven to 350°F (175°C).

2. Mix all the ingredients together.

3. Spoon the ingredients into a non-stick loaf tin, spread evenly, and bake it for 60 to 65 minutes.

4. Cool on a wire rack, slice, and serve!

School meals in Ghana

It is difficult to work hard at school if you are hungry or if the food you eat is not good for you. The Tibung School in Ghana, Africa, is working to provide students with healthy meals that are also good for the local **environment** and the planet.

Case study—School meals at the Tibung School

The students at Tibung School in Ghana, Africa, have made a commitment to eat in a **green** way. They eat corn, yams, rice, okra, and meat from local farms. Eggs, tomatoes, and onions are brought in from the nearest town.

These children are waiting for lunch in Tibung, Ghana.

Sylvia

10-year-old Sylvia says:

"My favorite food is rice and beans! The portions of the meals we get in school are big enough, but I finish it all! In my class, we have about 36 children and we eat the meals in our classroom."

School feeding program

The Dutch organization SIGN is donating money to schools in Ghana, such as Tibung, to help the schools provide hot meals for children. The children get a healthy meal and the food is provided by local farmers.

Challenge!

Find out where the food for school lunches comes from. Ask your school to buy as much food as possible from local farmers or farmers' markets if you live in an urban area. The food is often organic, which is better for you and the environment.

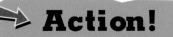

Action!

The whole school can help make meals healthy and green.

Write a letter to your principal to try to persuade him or her to only buy local, healthy produce for school meals.

Gladys

Gladys Abaa, teacher at Tibung School says:

"I eat with the children in the classroom. The food is nutritious and good, and it encourages children to come to school... the attention of the children is also better!"

From farm to fork

Local farmer Francis Kwaku will provide Tibung School with rice, corn, and groundnuts.

Francis Kwaku says:

Francis

"I sell my produce to the markets nearby. My farm is located approximately 7.5 miles (12 km) from the school, where one of my children attends as well."

A school store

Healthy snacks help to give you energy. Choose healthy snacks at home and at school. Some schools run **eco-friendly** stores that sell healthy snacks to students to help keep them going all day long.

Healthy school store

If your school has a garden, you can grow fruits and vegetables to sell at the school store. The money you make can go toward looking after the garden.

Mossbank School in Shetland sells food to students that was grown at the school. These treats were made for Halloween.

Chocolate

Dora

Soda

Chips

Chips

Dora has replaced chips, chocolate, and cans of soda with healthy snacks, such as fruit, that do not come in packaging.

This poster has a catch phrase to help sell the food. Think of some more catchy phrases to sell your school store food.

Running a store

Buy fruits and vegetables from local farmers and Fairtrade suppliers. Sell whole fruit, fruit slices, cups of vegetable sticks, homemade smoothies, and banana bread (see page 9).

Smoothie recipe
- Half a blender of fruit juice or a quarter juice and a quarter milk
- 1 peeled, chopped banana
- A handful of other chopped fruit
- Add a little honey or yogurt

Blend it all up together and enjoy a healthy drink.

Run your own school store
Give everyone at school the chance to snack on healthy, eco-friendly food.

Promoting your store
Make posters to promote the store. Make sure they tell people about the delicious and healthy snacks for sale, and about the eco-benefits of the store.

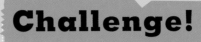

Action!

Do some market research.
Send out a questionnaire to parents, staff, and students. Ask:
- Would you buy snacks from a school store?
- How much would you pay for a snack?
- What would you like to eat?

Use the answers to decide how to set up the store.

Choose suppliers of local, organic, or Fairtrade fruits and vegetables.

A school garden

All around the world, schools are creating their own gardens. Schools grow healthy food to cook and eat. There is sometimes enough left over to sell and make money for looking after their gardens. Making sure their gardens are eco-friendly has helped many schools to become eco-schools. Rocklands Primary is a great example of an eco-school.

Zita

At Rocklands Primary, a small school in Mitchell's Plain, South Africa, Mrs. Zita Cheemee and her students have created a fantastic vegetable and wildlife garden. Every morning, children water the plants, weed the garden, and empty leftover food into a composting "bath."

Food from your own garden does not need extra packaging.

Action!

Eat healthy and help to look after your environment.

- Grow your own fruits and vegetables.
- Food from your own garden does not have far to travel to your plate.
- Recycle food waste to make your own compost.
- Avoid using chemicals by controlling pests naturally. Onions, garlic, and chillies will do the job.
- Save water by collecting rainwater to water the garden.

To teach students about how their food choices affect their health, the environment, and the **community** they live in, chef Alice Waters created the edible school garden at Martin Luther King Junior Middle School, California. Students learn in an organic garden and kitchen classroom.

Case study— The edible school garden

To make a change from buying food in the supermarket, the Martin Luther King Junior Middle School, in California, has created an **edible** school garden. The children sow the seeds and look after the growing plants.

Students learn about healthy eating and caring for the environment. They get plenty of outdoor fun and exercise at the same time.

Local and seasonal food

It is possible to grow food in most parts of the world all year round. You will not need a greenhouse or extra lighting, heating, and water for seasonal crops to thrive. They will be extra tasty, too.

Challenge!

You can harvest food from your garden all year round.

When you are planning your school garden, find out which fruits and vegetables grow well where you live and the best time to plant and harvest them.

Here are some popular fruits and vegetables. Find out when you have to sow and harvest them:

- Leeks
- Broccoli
- Peas
- Pumpkin
- Strawberries
- Tomatoes

How far has it traveled?

The food on this plate comes from all over the world. The vegetables come from Spain and Kenya, the potatoes from the United States, and the beef comes from Argentina. Where does your food come from?

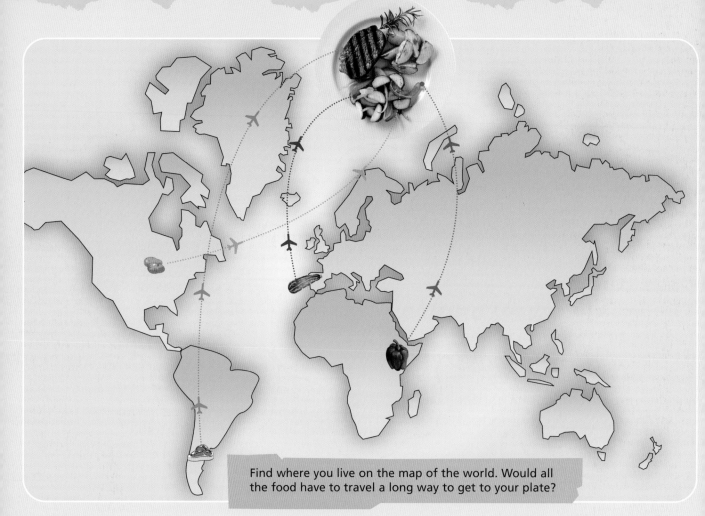

Find where you live on the map of the world. Would all the food have to travel a long way to get to your plate?

Food miles

Food miles are the distance food has to travel from the farm to your plate. Much of the food we eat travels from place to place by air, water, and land. The further food has to travel, the more fuel is used and more damage is done to the environment.

Local markets

In many places in the world, farmers bring their food to sell at the local market. Most of the customers come on foot because they live nearby. Food from the market does not have far to travel to make a delicious meal of fresh food to put on the table.

Challenge!

Work out the food miles.

- Add up the food miles of your own lunch.
- Add up the food miles of your friend's lunch.
- Which of you can change your lunch and have the fewest food miles?

Go to **www.organiclinker.com/food-miles** for a food miles calculator.

Eric →

At this market in Tanzania, women sell the vegetables they grow on their small farms.

Eric lives in New York. The bread in his lunch box was made from wheat grown in Minnesota, the apple came from Florida, and the peanuts from South Africa. What is the food mileage on his lunch? How could he improve it?

Action!

Cutting down food miles

- Walk to the store to buy your food.
- Whenever you can, buy local food. Shop at a farmers' market.
- Find out where food comes from and how far it has traveled.
- Find out if your school meals are cooked from local, fresh food. If not, see if you can make changes.

Get cooking!

Food you have grown yourself tastes especially good. If you have a garden at home, ask if you can have a small patch to grow vegetables. Treat your family to a meal you have cooked with vegetables from your garden.

Case study—Nunawading School

Nunawading School in Australia works with the Stephanie Alexander Kitchen Garden Foundation to encourage children to grow, harvest, prepare, and share their own food.

Challenge!

Find out what you can grow where you live so you have fresh food all year round.

- Grow it.
- Harvest it.
- Learn how to cook it.
- Eat it!

1. Students grow vegetables such as runner beans, tomatoes, and cucumbers in the school garden.

 Aaron, 7, says:

"I love planting vegetables and watching them grow through the year. Best of all is when we get to pick them and make delicious meals from them. It is good to know where our food comes from."

2. Students then pick the produce and take it into the kitchen, supervised by adults.

3. Delicious meals are then served for the rest of the school.

Weerayut

Weerayut, 10, says:

"I enjoy working in the vegetable garden. Thanks to this project, I have learned about vegetables, how to grow them, and to look after chickens. My family now asks for my advice and help and I know I can contribute."

Case study—A vegetable garden in Thailand

The Ban-Daeng School in Mahasarakham, Thailand, has more than 150 students and serves five neighboring villages. The school, local farmers, and the charity Plan International have introduced a vegetable garden and farm into the school.

Using the vegetables

Through the management of the school vegetable garden and a small farm, the students learned how to raise livestock and grow vegetables.

People use the fresh produce to prepare healthy lunches for the students, reducing the malnutrition rate. People sell the remainder of the produce to market sellers and community members.

The students of Ban-Daeng School in Thailand made a delicious pak choi salad using local ingredients.

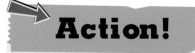

Action!

Get cooking!

Make a delicious salad like the one on the right using fresh ingredients from your local area.

Crispy lettuce, spring onions, peas, and apple make up this green salad.

Mini gardens

Your home might not have a garden and many schools do not have space for a garden. You can still grow all kinds of different fruits and vegetables in window boxes, pots, hanging baskets, and containers.

What can you grow?

You can grow almost anything. Start with food you like to eat. Grow just one or two vegetables at first. When you get good at it, try something new.

These old tires have been used for growing potatoes!

Some vegetables, such as chives, grow in very small spaces.

Inside and outside

Window sills are good places for growing small pots of herbs. Sunlight shines through the glass and you can open the windows for some fresh air. Remember to water the pots. The rain cannot do the job for you inside!

Outside, unused containers can act as places for growing food. Old tires, pots, and even old boots are all ideal places to grow different kinds of plants.

Challenge!

Use your imagination

Do not buy new containers, reuse what you already have:

- half an old football for a hanging basket
- plastic storage boxes
- baskets
- old boots

The container must:

- be big enough for the fully grown plant
- have holes for water to drain

Fill it with eco-friendly soil.
Use homemade compost (see pages 22-23).

Seeds can be planted in any container, from an old football to a hanging basket.

Action!

Prepare a container.

- Punch holes for drainage.
- Add light soil. Make sure it is clean and fresh. Try to use soil without **peat**.
- Water the soil.
- Plant a young vegetable or fruit plant.
- If your container is light, you can move it to protect it from the hot sun or a frost.

Looking after containers

Containers need some shelter and some sunshine. They can stand against a wall or fence. Put them close to a hose so you can water them easily and keep your gardening tools handy. If you are using a window box, make sure it is firmly fixed to the window sill.

Pete

Children at Pete's school take the containers home and water the vegetables on weekends and during holidays.

Compost

Soil is made up of tiny bits of rock, dead plants, and animals. Plants take nutrients from the soil to feed them as they grow. Soil that is used for growing vegetables over and over again loses some of its nutrients. It needs feeding with good quality compost.

You can make your own compost at home or at school. The children at Rocklands Primary in South Africa have created a compost "bath," and use earthworms to turn leftover food into great compost.

What is compost?

Compost is decayed plants and other natural things such as tea leaves or fruit and vegetable peels. It is added to soil to make the soil richer.

Compost helps keep soil full of the nutrients plants need to grow healthy.

You can add certain school lunch leftovers to your school compost heap.

Why is a compost heap green?

Compost heaps:
- reduce waste
- recycle food
- make natural compost
- help vegetables to grow
- help you grow strong and healthy when you eat the vegetables

Fruits and vegetables, like these old pumpkins, make great compost.

What can be made into compost?

- Uncooked fruit and vegetable leftovers, such as peels, cores, and pits. Put in bread and tea leaves, too.
- Do not put meat, fish, or cheese into your compost—they can attract rats and other pests.

! Peat compost

Peat is formed naturally from rotted plants and is found in peat bogs. Once peat has been dug up for compost, it will take many years for it to form again. It is much better to make your own compost than use peat compost.

Sara and Marié's school in France has started using a new compost bin to dispose of the students' unwanted food.

Sara   Marié

Action!

Make compost

- You will need a compost bin with a lid. The bin has no bottom and should be placed flat on soil to allow worms and other insects to get in.
- Add a mixture of uncooked food waste, leaves, grass clippings, and weeds.
- Mix with egg boxes and brown paper. It will start to rot and get hot.
- Worms and beetles will start to break down the contents of your bin.
- When rich, dark brown compost develops at the bottom, it can be used in the garden to make soil rich.

Safety

Wear gloves. Wash your hands.

Fairtrade

Cheap food for us can mean that farmers in poor parts of the developing world are not getting a fair price for their food. Fairtrade products avoid this. They are sometimes more expensive. This is because the farmers have been given enough money to pay their workers a good wage to live on.

FAIRTRADE

The Fairtrade logo on food in our stores tells us that the farmers who produced the food are getting a **fair deal** when we buy it. Look for the Fairtrade logo when you go shopping.

Fairtrade produce

Fairtrade food you can buy includes fresh fruit, cocoa, chocolate, sugar, coffee, tea, rice, herbs and spices, honey, nuts, and snacks.

This farmer produces Fairtrade bananas. They are sold in supermarkets all over the world.

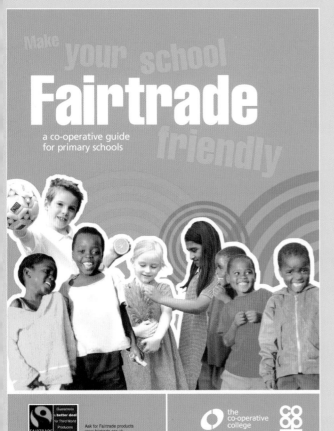

Get your school to become a Fairtrade school by only buying Fairtrade products.

Rich/poor lunch

A rich/poor lunch will help you learn the concept of "fair" and "unfair." Everyone buys a numbered ticket for the same price. Tickets are pulled out of a hat. Some children get a slice of pizza and something sweet for dessert, while others just get a small bowl of rice and beans. Think about the fact that in some parts of the world, people have to survive on a "poor lunch" every day of their lives. Is this fair?

rich lunch

poor lunch

Challenge!

- Recognize the Fairtrade products logo.
- Change something you buy regularly to a Fairtrade product.
- Add more Fairtrade food to your shopping basket week by week and eat it in your lunch.
- Challenge your school to buy Fairtrade food for school lunches and the staff room.

Food festival

Holding a food festival is a way to share all you have learned about what is good for you and good for the planet with friends, family, other schools, and the local community. Plan a festival that will inspire everyone to think about the food they eat and then make changes at home, at school, or at the places they work.

Action!

At your food festival:

- Sell cakes, bread, and smoothies made by a cooking club.
- Give a cooking demonstration.
- Set up a stall with posters and information about Fairtrade and food miles.
- Sell produce from the school garden.
- Give guided tours of the vegetable garden.
- Invite everyone to share an eco-friendly school lunch.
- Have competitions, games, and workshops.

Food festivals

These children in Morocco are taking part in a food festival. They are making food from all over the world for other people to eat and enjoy. This encourages others to see where food comes from and what good food should taste like.

Challenge!

- Hold a food festival.
- Invite people from the local community and family and friends.
- Plan a day of fun that everyone will remember.
- Follow it up and find out if anyone has made changes to the way they grow, buy, cook, and eat their food.

Learn about food

Local farmers and organic and Fairtrade food suppliers often set up stalls at festivals and introduce themselves to the local community. This is a great way to learn more about good food.

Cooking demonstration

Cooking clubs sometimes offer demonstrations of their favorite eco-friendly recipes. You could go along and get a chance to taste the food and learn how to make it at home.

This picture shows a local farmers' market in the United States

Fun at cooking club!

Nutrition from your neighborhood

Use foods grown locally—it's good for you and for the world.

Let's Get Started!

Eating nutritious foods is important. It's also important to know where your food comes from. Try to choose foods that are grown or raised nearby. Otherwise, a lot of coal or oil is burned by vehicles bringing you foods from faraway places. Local foods use less energy to get to your dinner table.

Choosing foods with little or no packaging or with recyclable packaging is also smart. Local foods often need less packaging than foods that travel a long way.

In this project, you will plan and prepare a recipe that uses local foods. Then, with your classmates, you will write and distribute a cookbook with recipes based on local foods.

Activity

1. Visit a library and find information about foods that are grown or raised in your area. Look in books, magazines, or online. In many places there is a county extension office. This agency offers information about local agricultural products. If you need help, you can ask a librarian.

2. Choose a few recipes that have some local ingredients, according to your research. List the ingredients. Picking a few different recipes is a good idea because some ingredients might not be easily available, even if they're grown locally.

3. With an adult, visit a local farmers' market. Farmers' markets sell fruits and vegetables that are grown locally and meat that is raised locally.

You might also find flour made from locally grown grain or dairy products made from local cows' milk. If there is no farmers' market where you live, go to a grocery store. Keep in mind what types of foods are grown locally and look for those. Don't forget to bring your list of ingredients and reusable shopping bags!

4. Once you see what foods are for sale at the farmers' market, choose a recipe that uses some local products. Buy the foods you need for the recipe.

5. Prepare your recipe for your family, using the local foods you purchased. Ask an adult to help you use the stove and other electrical appliances.

6. Write a "local foods" cookbook with your classmates. Include the recipes everyone prepared. Think of a good title for the cover. The title should include the name of your town. It should also tell readers that the recipes inside are based on local ingredients. Make copies of the cookbook and distribute them at a farmers' market.

Looking Back

Discuss your experiences with your classmates.

- Which foods did you find from your ingredients list? Which foods didn't you find?

- How did the foods taste compared to the same foods purchased at a grocery store?

- How do you think your purchases helped your community?

Plan a "local foods day" for your class. You and your classmates can prepare dishes to bring in and share.

Glossary

Community
A community is all the people who live and work in a neighborhood. Some communities are big and other communities are small.

Compost
Compost is decayed plants, food waste, and paper rotted down together and dug into soil to make it richer.

Eco-friendly
Eco-friendly means not being harmful to the environment or to the plants and animals that live in it.

Edible
Edible means something you can eat.

Environment
The environment is everything around you. You might live in a built-up environment, such as a city, or in a natural environment such as the countryside.

Fair deal
A fair deal is an agreement people come to when they are buying and selling. A fair deal is one in which both sides get fair treatment.

Green
We call protecting the planet we live on and looking after the environment being "green."

Green Team
A school Green Team is a group of children and staff who work together to protect the planet and the environment.

Organic
Things that are organic have been alive. Garden clippings, food waste, and wood are all organic. Organic food is food grown with severely restricted use of pesticides and chemical fertilizers. Animals are raised without the routine use of drugs and antibiotics common in intensive livestock farming.

Peat
Peat is made up of dead plants including bog moss and is found in bogs. It is dug up and burned for fuel or made into compost.

Recycled
Things that are recycled are made of materials that can be used again. Plastic, glass, metal, and paper are all materials that can be recycled, some more easily than others.

Seasonal
Seasonal food is ready to be eaten at certain times of the year because of the temperature and the weather. Food that is grown in glass houses can be ready to eat regardless of the weather and temperature.

Websites

www.eco-schools.org
Your school can become part of an international group of schools committed to caring for the environment.

www.fairtrade.org
Fairtrade promotes fair deals for farmers. Find out why you might choose to become a Fairtrade school and how to go about it.

www.thefoodtrust.org
Information about healthy eating and improving school food.

www.canadianfoodsafetyinstitute.ca
Find out about the food you buy, food labels, organic food, and support available for schools.

www.foecanada.og
An animation with plenty of useful information about the food we eat.

www.edenproject.com
The Eden Project focuses on our relationship with plants. Learn about the plants we eat and how to enjoy eating them.

www.edibleschoolyard.org
Students in California learn how to grow, harvest, and prepare nutritious seasonal produce. They find out about the natural world and the environmental and social well-being of their school community.

Index

Printed in China